the Children's
food & drink party book

R&R PUBLICATIONS MARKETING PTY LTD

R&R Publications Marketing Pty Ltd
12 Edward Street, Brunswick
Victoria 3056, Australia
Phone (61 3) 9381 2199 Fax (61 3) 9381 2689
Australia-wide toll free 1800 063 296
E-mail: info@randrpublications.com.au
Web: www.randrpublications.com.au
©Richard Carroll 2006

Publisher: Richard Carroll
Designer: Aisling Gallagher
Food Editor: Neil Hargreaves
Photographer: Brent Parker Jones
Food Stylist: Neil Hargreaves
Presentation: R&R PhotoStudio
Proofreader: Sandra Goldbloom Zurbo

ISBN: 1 74022 571 6
EAN: 9 781740 225717

Published: October 2006
Printed in China by
Max Production Printing Ltd

Cover image: Strawberry Swirl, page 81

Contents

Smoothie Origins

Many of the drinks in *The Children's food and party book* are smoothie-style drinks. Smoothies deserve a quick introduction.

Smoothies, a drink made of fruit and, often, yoghurt and honey are reminiscent of traditional old-world drinks of India and the Middle East. Many early Hindu offerings in drink form contain honey and yoghurt. So, the smoothie has been around in different forms for a long time.

Earliest known smoothie recipes in the West date back to Los Angeles in the 1920s, but it wasn't until the 1970s that smoothies began to be seen as a healthy alternative to milkshakes – being primarily fresh fruit based, and sometimes containing a little milk and yoghurt, not all dairy, including ice cream, and flavoured syrups. By the 1990s, smoothie bars could be found everywhere.

In *The Children's food and party book*, we have started with a few simple classics to get you rolling, fruit combinations that are very popular at smoothie bars and juice bars. These are followed by more novel and festive recipes that are fun and playful combinations for the day of the party.

The Children's food and party book finishes up with more complicated combinations, recipes for the older and more adventurous children and the young at heart. After all, why should the kids have all the fun!

Getting Organised

Take the time to taste your first drink, particularly if you are making a few batches for a party of children, and remember to adjust the amount of sweeteners you are using. This will depend upon the season. Most fruits are sweeter at different times of the year; they are more luscious and hold more moisture when they are in season. It is worth having a look at the markets to see what is on offer and be guided by what is abundant at the time. Not only will your fruit be sweeter but it will taste better and be cheaper when it is in season.

In most of these recipes you can easily add more ice to mellow out the flavours and make your drinks go further or, for a stronger flavoured slushie-style of drink, you can deseed and peel your fruits, then cut them into ice-sized cubes. Do this ahead of time. Lay them out in the freezer (on trays or in ice trays rather than bowls so they do not end up as one large block when frozen). This bit of extra planning keeps you more organised and cleaner. You can freeze your fruits a long way ahead of time and even prepare and freeze fruit that will be out of season on the day of the party.

Raspberry Orange Delight (page 78)

Fruit Combo's

Banana Smoothie 14
Banapple Smoothie 14
Banberry Smoothie 14
Berry Banana Smoothie 19
Banana Zing Smoothie 19
Calypso Smoothie 19
Custard Apple Smoothie 22
Fruit Salad Smoothie 22
Grape Slushie Swirl 22
Hawaiian Delight Smoothie 27
Kiwi Frootz Smoothie 27
Mango and Orange Smoothie 27
Mango Morning Smoothie 30
Melon Mix Smoothie 30
Passion Frootz 30
Strawberry Orange Banana Smoothie 35
Strawberry Smoothie 35
Sunrise Surprise Smoothie 35
Tropical Burst Smoothie 38
Tropical Frootz Smoothie 38
Tropical Zing Smoothie 38
Tropicana Smoothie 43
Tropico Blitz 43

Banana Smoothie

½ cup milk
1½ bananas
½ cup plain yoghurt
1 tsp honey

2–3 drops vanilla essence
sprinkle of nutmeg (optional)
4 ice cubes

Place all ingredients except nutmeg in blender; blend until smooth. Pour into chilled glasses and serve topped with a sprinkle of nutmeg. Serves 2.

Banapple Smoothie

½ cup milk
½ banana
½ apple, peeled
½ cup plain yoghurt

1 tsp honey
2–3 drops vanilla essence
3 ice cubes
purple sprinkles to garnish

Place all ingredients except sprinkles in blender; blend until smooth. Pour into chilled glasses and serve. Serves 2.

Banberry Smoothie

½ cup milk
½ banana
2 strawberries
½ apple, peeled

5–6 blueberries
½ cup plain yoghurt
1 tsp honey
3 ice cubes

Place all ingredients in blender; blend until smooth, Pour into chilled glasses and serve topped with coloured sprinkles. Serves 2.

Banana Smoothie

Banapple Smoothie

Banberry Smoothie

Berry Banana Smoothie

Berry Banana Smoothie

½ cup milk
1 banana
6 frozen strawberries
10–12 blueberries

1 tsp honey
2 drops of vanilla essence
vanilla sugar
4 ice cubes

Place all ingredients except sugar in blender; blend until smooth. Pour into chilled glasses and serve topped with a fresh strawberry, a few blueberries and a sprinkle of vanilla sugar. Serves 2.

Banana Zing Smoothie

½ cup milk
½ banana
juice of 1 orange
3–4 drops lemon juice

½ cup plain yoghurt
2 tsps apple juice concentrate
2 slices of orange
4 ice cubes

Place all ingredients except orange slices in blender; blend until smooth. Pour into chilled glasses and serve topped with a slice of orange. Serves 2.

Calypso Smoothie

½ cup milk
⅓ cup pineapple
pulp of 2 passionfruit
½ banana

½ cup plain yoghurt
1 tsp honey
extra passionfruit pulp to garnish
4 ice cubes

Place all ingredients, except garnish in blender; blend until smooth. Pour into chilled glasses and serve with a swirl of passionfruit to garnish. Serves 2.

Custard Apple Smoothie

½ cup milk
½ cup custard apple, deseeded
½ banana
½ cup plain yoghurt

1 tsp honey
2 drops vanilla essence
nutmeg
4 ice cubes

Place all ingredients, except nutmeg in blender; blend until smooth. Pour into chilled glasses and serve topped with a sprinkle of nutmeg. Serves 2.

Fruit Salad Smoothie

½ cup milk
⅓ cup of pineapple
2 strawberries
⅓ banana

⅓ apple, peeled
½ cup plain yoghurt
1 tsp honey
4 ice cubes

Place all ingredients in blender; blend until smooth. Pour into chilled glasses and serve. Serves 2.

Grape Slushie Swirl

1 cup seedless red grapes, frozen
1 cup seedless green grapes, frozen
¼ tsp fresh ginger pulp

2 tbsps fig jam
1 tsp white sugar
2 ice blocks

Blend 1 ice block, green grapes, ginger pulp and sugar in blender until slushy and all combined. Spoon out into a chilled bowl and place in freezer. Blend the other ice block, red grapes and fig jam until slushy and all combined. Spoon out into a chilled bowl. Collect green grape slushie and spoon each coloured mixture into serving glasses, a few scoops of each colour at a time until glasses are full. Serves 2.

Custard Apple Smoothie

Fruit Salad Smoothie

Grape Slushie Swirl

Hawaiian Delight Smoothie

Hawaiian Delight Smoothie

½ cup milk
6 cherries
½ cup pineapple
½ mandarin
½ cup plain yoghurt

1 tsp honey
2–3 drops vanilla essence
pink sprinkles
2 ice cubes

Place all ingredients except sprinkles in blender; blend until smooth.
Pour into chilled glasses and serve topped with coloured sprinkles.
Serves 2.

Kiwi Frootz Smoothie

½ cup milk
½ banana
2 frozen strawberries
1½ peeled kiwifruit
½ cup plain yoghurt

2 tsps honey
4 ice cubes
extra kiwifruit and banana to garnish
½ tsp vanilla sugar

Place all ingredients except garnish in blender; blend until smooth.
Pour into chilled glasses and serve topped with a slice of fresh
kiwifruit and banana. Serves 2.

Mango and Orange Smoothie

½ cup milk
pulp of 1 mango
juice of 1 orange
½ cup plain yoghurt

1 tsp honey
pinch of cinnamon
2 ice cubes

Place all ingredients except cinnamon in blender; blend until
smooth. Pour into chilled glasses and serve topped with a sprinkle of
cinnamon. Serves 2.

Kiwi Frootz Smoothie

Mango and Orange Smoothie

Mango Morning Smoothie

½ cup milk
½ mango
¼ banana
½ cup plain yoghurt

2 tsps toasted muesli
1 tbsp date paste
3 ice cubes

Place all ingredients in blender; blend until smooth. Pour into chilled glasses and serve topped with a sprinkle of muesli. Serves 2.

Melon Mix Smoothie

¼ cup milk
⅓ banana
½ cup watermelon, deseeded
½ cup rock melon or cantaloupe

½ cup plain yoghurt
1 tsp honey
2–3 drops vanilla essence
3 ice cubes

Freeze melons. Place all other ingredients in blender; blend until smooth. Pour into chilled glasses and serve topped with chunks of frozen melon. Serves 2.

Passion Frootz

½ cup milk
½ apple
½ banana
juice of 1 orange

pulp of 1 passionfruit
½ cup plain yoghurt
extra passionfruit pulp to garnish
1 tsp honey

Place all ingredients except garnish in blender; blend until smooth. Pour into chilled glasses and serve topped with a swirl of passionfruit pulp. Serves 2.

Mango Morning Smoothie

Melon Mix Smoothie

Passion Frootz

Strawberry Orange Banana Smoothie

Strawberry ✩ Orange Banana Smoothie

½ cup milk

1 orange, peeled and deseeded

½ banana

2 strawberries

½ cup plain yoghurt

1 tsp honey

2–3 drops vanilla essence

2 ice cubes

Place all ingredients in blender; blend until smooth. Pour into chilled glasses and serve. Serves 2.

Strawberry Smoothie

½ cup milk

6 frozen strawberries

½ cup plain yoghurt

1 tsp honey

2–3 drops vanilla essence

pinch of nutmeg (optional)

extra strawberry to garnish

4 blocks of ice

Place all ingredients except garnish in blender; blend until smooth. Pour into chilled glasses and serve topped with half a fresh strawberry. Serves 2.

Sunrise Surprise Smoothie

1 blood orange, peeled and deseeded

pulp of ½ mango

pulp of 2 passionfruit

½ cup plain yoghurt

1 tsp honey

2–3 drops vanilla essence

extra yoghurt and passionfruit to garnish

4 ice cubes

Place all ingredients except garnishes in blender; blend until smooth. Pour into chilled glasses and serve topped with an extra dollop of yoghurt and some passionfruit pulp. Serves 2.

Strawberry Smoothie

Sunrise Surprise Smoothie

Tropical Burst Smoothie

¼ cup milk
1 kiwifruit, peeled and quartered
3 strawberries
½ cup of watermelon, deseeded
½ cup plain yoghurt
1 tsp honey
2 ice cubes

Place all ingredients in blender; blend until smooth. Pour into chilled glasses and serve. Serves 2.

Tropical Frootz Smoothie

½ cup milk
½ banana
2 strawberries
½ cup pineapple
½ cup plain yoghurt

1 tsp honey
½ cup coconut milk
extra strawberries to garnish
2 ice cubes

Place all ingredients except garnish in blender; blend until smooth. Pour in ½ cup of coconut milk and stir. Pour into chilled glasses and serve topped with strawberries. Serves 2.

Tropical Zing Smoothie

⅓ cup milk
½ orange
¼ mango
pulp of 2 passionfruit

½ cup pineapple
½ cup plain yoghurt
1 tsp honey
2 ice cubes

Reserve some passionfruit. Place all other ingredients in blender; blend until smooth. Pour into chilled glasses and serve topped with passionfruit. Serves 2.

Tropical Burst Smoothie

Tropical Frootz Smoothie

Tropical Zing Smoothie

Tropicana Smoothie

Tropicana Smoothie

½ cup milk
½ mango
½ banana
½ apple
2 strawberries
extra strawberry to garnish
¼ cup plain yoghurt
1 tsp honey
3 ice cubes

Place all ingredients except garnish in blender; blend until smooth.
Pour into chilled glasses and serve topped with a fanned strawberry.
Serves 2.

Tropico Blitz

1 small ripe banana, sliced
1 cup frozen peach slices
½ cup orange juice
2 tbsps fresh lime juice
2 tbsps honey
4 drops vanilla extract
¼ tsp ground cinnamon
2 ice blocks

Place all ingredients except cinnamon in blender; blend until
smooth. Pour into chilled glasses and serve topped with a sprinkle of
cinnamon. Serves 2.

Tropico Blitz

Novelty Drinks

Anzac Cookie Smoothie **46**
Apple Cherry Pie Smoothie **46**
Apple Crumble Smoothie **46**
Apricot Danish Smoothie **51**
Banana Berry Muffin Smoothie **51**
Banana Cherry Split Smoothie **51**
Banana Choc Nut Smoothie **54**
Banana Pudding Smoothie **54**
Banario Smoothie **54**
Cheesecake Smoothie **59**
Cherry Ripe Smoothie **59**
Choc Berry Smoothie **59**
Choc Mint Berry Smoothie **62**
Honey Smack Smoothie **62**
Honeydew Heaven **62**
Iced Vovo Smoothie **67**
Jaffa Smoothie **67**
Lemon Meringue Smoothie **67**
Lucious Lime Pie Smoothie **70**
Monte Carlo Smoothie **70**
Muesli Bar Smoothie **70**
Peanut Butter and Jam Smoothie **75**
Pear and Coconut Delight Smoothie **75**
Pear Danish Smoothie **75**
Raspberry Orange Delight **78**
Strawberry Shortcake Smoothie **78**
Strawberry Swirl **81**
Toffee Apple Smoothie **81**

Anzac Cookie Smoothie

½ cup milk
½ cup plain yoghurt
½ cup stewed or roasted pear,
 chilled
½ cup toasted muesli

extra toasted muesli to garnish
2 tsps golden syrup
3 drops of vanilla essence
3 ice cubes

Place all ingredients except garnish in blender; blend until smooth. Pour into chilled glasses and serve topped with extra muesli. Serves 2.

Apple Cherry Pie Smoothie

½ cup milk
2 strawberries
3 cherries, pipes removed
½ apple skinned
½ tsp apple juice concentrate
½ cup plain yoghurt

1 tsp caramel syrup
dash of nutmeg
dash of cinnamon
2 drops of vanilla essence
2 tsp cinnamon sugar
3 ice cubes

Place all ingredients except cinnamon in blender; blend until smooth. Pour into chilled glasses and serve topped with cinnamon sugar. Serves 2.

Apple Crumble Smoothie

½ cup milk
½ custard apple, pipes removed
½ banana
½ cup plain yoghurt
1 tsp caramel sauce

¼ cup toasted muesli
sprinkle of cinnamon and nutmeg
2 drops vanilla essence
1 tbsp coconut
3 ice cubes

Place all ingredients except coconut in blender; blend until smooth. Pour into chilled glasses and serve topped with toasted coconut. Serves 2.

Anzac Cookie Smoothie

Apple Cherry Pie Smoothie

Apple Crumble Smoothie

Apricot Danish Smoothie

Apricot Danish Smoothie

¼ cup milk
½ cup stewed or roasted apricots, chilled
¼ cup plain yoghurt
¼ cup Philadelphia cream cheese
¼ cup apricot nectar

½ tsp honey
2–3 drops vanilla essence
dash of nutmeg
dash of cinnamon
4 ice cubes

Place all ingredients except spices in blender; blend until smooth. Pour into chilled glasses and serve topped with cinnamon and nutmeg. Serves 2.

Banana Berry Muffin Smoothie

½ cup milk
½ banana
12 blueberries
½ cup plain yoghurt
2 tsps toffee sauce

2 tsps ground almond spread
2–3 drops vanilla essence
pinch of cinnamon and nutmeg
extra blueberries to garnish
4 ice cubes

Place all ingredients in blender; blend until smooth. Pour into chilled glasses and serve topped with a scatter of blueberries. Serves 2.

Banana Cherry Split Smoothie

½ cup milk
1 banana
6 cherries, pips removed
1 tbsp strawberry jam
1 tbsp chocolate syrup

½ cup plain yoghurt
2–3 drops vanilla essence
small chocolate buttons to garnish
4 ice cubes

Place all ingredients except garnish in blender; blend until smooth. Pour into chilled glasses and serve topped with chocolate buttons. Serves 2.

Banana Berry Muffin Smoothie

Banana Cherry Split Smoothie

Banana Choc Nut Smoothie

½ cup milk
1 banana
2 tbsp chocolate sauce
2 tbsp hazelnut paste
½ cup plain yoghurt

1 tsp honey
2–3 drops vanilla essence
pinch of nutmeg
4 ice cubes

Place all ingredients except nutmeg in blender; blend until smooth.
Pour into chilled glasses and serve topped with nutmeg. Serves 2.

Banana Pudding Smoothie

½ cup milk
1 banana
½ cup plain yoghurt
½ tsp caramel sauce
½ tsp toffee sauce

2–3 drops vanilla essence
4 ice cubes
1 tbsp toasted coconut
pinch of nutmeg

Place all ingredients in blender; blend until smooth. Pour into chilled
glasses and serve topped with toasted coconut. Serves 2.

Banario Smoothie

½ cup milk
1 banana
2 Oreo biscuits, crushed

⅓ cup plain yoghurt
4 ice cubes
extra biscuit, crushed to garnish

Place all ingredients except garnish in blender; blend until smooth.
Pour into chilled glasses and serve topped with half an Oreo or
chocolate biscuit. Serves 2.

Banana Choc Nut Smoothie

Banana Pudding Smoothie

Banario Smoothie

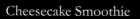

Cheesecake Smoothie

Cheesecake Smoothie

½ cup milk
½ cup custard apple, seeds removed
¼ cup Philadelphia cream
  cheese
¼ cup plain yoghurt
1 tsp caramel syrup

2 tsps hazelnut spread
2 drops vanilla essence
sprinkle of nutmeg
extra caramel syrup to garnish
4 ice cubes

Place all ingredients except topping in blender; blend until smooth.
Pour into chilled glasses and serve topped with a swirl of caramel
syrup. Serves 2.

Cherry Ripe Smoothie

10 frozen cherries, depipped
½ cup plain yoghurt
½ cup coconut milk

2 tsps dark chocolate sauce
2 ice cubes

Place all ingredients except toppings in blender; blend until smooth.
Pour in ½ cup of coconut milk and stir. Pour into chilled glasses and
serve topped with a cherry and a swirl of chocolate sauce. Serves 2.

Choc Berry Smoothie

½ cup milk
4 strawberries, frozen
8–10 blueberries
½ cup plain yoghurt
1 tbsp chocolate syrup

2–3 drops vanilla essence
extra chocolate syrup to garnish
1 extra strawberry to garnish
3 ice cubes

Place all ingredients in blender; blend until smooth. Pour into chilled
glasses and serve topped with half a strawberry and a swirl of syrup.
Serves 2.

Cherry Ripe Smoothie

Choc Berry Smoothie

Choc Mint Berry Smoothie

½ cup milk
½ banana
3 strawberries
2 tsps choc mint sauce

½ cup plain yoghurt
extra yoghurt to garnish
1 tsp strawberry jam
4 ice cubes

Place all ingredients except toppings in blender; blend until smooth. Pour into chilled glasses and serve topped with an extra yoghurt and coloured sprinkles. Serves 2.

Honey Smack Smoothie

½ cup milk
½ cup custard apple, deseeded
1 weetbix or ¾ cup
  frosted mini wheats
¼ cup plain yoghurt

2 tbsp honey
2–3 drops vanilla essence
extra cereal and honey
2 ice cubes

Place all ingredients except toppings in blender; blend until smooth. Pour into chilled glasses and serve topped with lots of crushed cereal and a dollop of honey. Serves 2.

Honeydew Heaven

½ cup diced honeydew
½ cup lime-flavoured drink
1 tsp lime juice

1 tbsp white sugar
1 large slice of cantaloupe, to garnish
6 ice cubes

Place all ingredients except lime soft drink and cantaloupe in blender; blend until smooth. Divide mixture between 2 glasses. Scoop out 3 to 4 balls of cantaloupe flesh, place in each glasses top up with lime-flavoured drink and give a gentle stir. Serves 2.

Choc Mint Berry Smoothie

Honey Smack Smoothie

Honeydew Heaven

Iced Vovo Smoothie

Iced Vovo Smoothie

½ cup milk
¼ cup coconut milk
½ custard apple, deseeded
2 strawberries
½ cup plain yoghurt

1 tsp raspberry jam
2 tsps macadamia paste
2 drops vanilla essence
toasted coconut to garnish
2 ice cubes

Place all ingredients except coconut in blender; blend until smooth. Pour into chilled glasses and serve topped with toasted coconut. Serves 2.

Jaffa Smoothie

¼ cup milk
½ banana
juice of 1 orange
½ cup plain yoghurt

2 tsps chocolate sauce
2–3 drops vanilla essence
chocolate curls for topping
2 ice cubes

Place all ingredients except topping in blender; blend until smooth. Pour into chilled glasses and serve topped with chocolate curls. Serves 2.

Lemon Meringue Smoothie

¼ cup milk
½ banana
2 tbsps lemon butter
2 tsps caramel sauce

½ cup plain yoghurt
2–3 drops vanilla essence
toasted coconut for topping
4 ice cubes

Place all ingredients except topping in blender; blend until smooth. Pour in ¼ cup of coconut milk and stir. Pour into chilled glasses and serve topped with toasted coconut. Serves 2.

Jaffa Smoothie

Lemon Meringue Smoothie

Luscious Lime Pie Smoothie

½ cup milk
1 kiwifruit, peeled
2 tbsps lemon butter
½ cup plain yoghurt
1 squeeze lime juice

1 tsp caramel sauce
2–3 drops vanilla essence
pinch of nutmeg
pinch of cinnamon
3 ice cubes

Place all ingredients except spices in blender; blend until smooth. Pour into chilled glasses and serve topped with a sprinkle of cinnamon and nutmeg. Serves 2.

Monte Carlo Smoothie

½ cup milk
½ custard apple, deseeded
½ banana
2 tsps macadamia paste
½ cup plain yoghurt

1 tsp raspberry jam
2–3 drops vanilla essence
sprinkle of nutmeg
1 crushed malt biscuit for topping
2 ice cubes

Place all ingredients except biscuit in blender; blend until smooth. Pour into chilled glasses and serve sprinkled with a crushed malt biscuit. Serves 2.

Muesli Bar Smoothie

½ cup milk
½ banana
2 tbsps muesli
2 tsps date pulp
½ cup plain yoghurt

½ tsp molasses
2–3 drops vanilla essence
extra muesli for topping
3 ice cubes

Place all ingredients except topping in blender; blend until smooth. Pour into chilled glasses and serve topped with a sprinkle of muesli. Serves 2.

Lucious Lime Pie Smoothie

Monte Carlo Smoothie

Muesli Bar Smoothie

Peanut Butter and Jam Smoothie

Peanut Butter and Jam Smoothie

½ cup milk
½ banana
4 strawberries
4 tbsps peanut butter

½ cup plain yoghurt
1 tsp strawberry jam
extra peanut butter for topping
4 ice cubes

Place all ingredients except topping in blender; blend until smooth. Pour into chilled glasses and serve topped with a dollop of peanut butter. Serves 2.

Pear and Coconut Delight Smoothie

½ cup milk
½ cup stewed or roasted pear, chilled
½ cup plain yoghurt
1 tsp honey
2 tbsps of toasted coconut

1 tsp pear concentrate
2 drops vanilla essence
extra yoghurt for topping
4 ice cubes

Place all ingredients except topping in blender; blend until smooth. Pour into chilled glasses and serve topped with an extra dollop of yoghurt and a sprinkle of toasted coconut. Serves 2.

Pear Danish Smoothie

½ cup milk
½ cup stewed or roasted pear, chilled
½ cup plain yoghurt
¼ cup Philadelphia cream cheese
½ tsp pear juice concentrate
½ tsp toffee-flavoured syrup

2–3 drops vanilla essence
1 Italian finger biscuit for topping
2 tsps honey
dash of nutmeg
4 ice cubes

Place all ingredients except biscuit, honey and nutmeg in blender; blend until smooth. Serve in chilled glasses, topped with crushed biscuit, an extra dollop of yoghurt and a drizzle of honey. Serves 2.

Pear and Coconut Delight Smoothie

Pear Danish Smoothie

Raspberry ✪range Delight (image page 12)

½ cup fresh or unsweetened frozen raspberries
½ cups orange juice
1 tbsps honey
½ cups lemon-lime soda
10 ice blocks

Blend raspberries, orange juice, honey. Put 5 ice blocks in each glass, add about half a cup of the raspberry mixture, then add a dash of the soda to each glasses.

Strawberry Shortcake Smoothie

½ cup milk
6–8 strawberries
½ cup plain yoghurt
1 tsp toffee-flavoured syrup
1 tsp caramel-flavoured syrup
2 drops vanilla essence
toasted coconut to garnish
dash of nutmeg
dash of cinnamon
4 ice cubes

Place all ingredients except spices and coconut in blender; blend until smooth. Pour into chilled glasses and serve topped with toasted coconut. Serves 2.

Strawberry Shortcake Smoothie

Black Forest Gateau Smoothie

¼ cup milk
¼ cup cream
½ cup plain yoghurt
3 tsps black cherry jam
1 tbsp chocolate syrup

3 cherries, pips removed
½ banana or ½ custard apple, deseeded
2–3 drops vanilla essence
chocolate curls
4 ice cubes

Place all ingredients except chocolate curls in blender; blend until smooth. Pour into chilled glasses and serve topped with a chocolate curls. Serves 2.

Cantaloupe Cooler

1 cup cantaloupe pieces
1 tbsp orange juice
1 tsp lemon juice

2 tsps white sugar
1 cup lemonade
2 ice blocks

Blend cantaloupe until liquefied. Pour half into tall glasses filled with ice and top up with lemonade. Serves 6.

Cherry Fruit Cake Smoothie

½ cup milk
¼ apple
4 blueberries
2 cherries
½ banana
½ cup plain yoghurt
½ tsp caramel sauce

½ tsp toffee-flavoured sauce
1 tbsp date spread
2 drops vanilla essence
extra berries for topping
dash of nutmeg
3 ice cubes

Place all ingredients except berries and nutmeg in blender; blend until smooth. Pour into chilled glasses and serve topped with berries. Serves 2.

Black Forest Gateau Smoothie

Cantaloupe Cooler

Cherry Fruit Cake Smoothie

Cranberry Zinger

Cranberry Zinger

½ cup cranberry juice
2 tsps brown sugar
1 tsp lemon extract
1 cup pineapple pieces (approximately 5oz/150g)
1 cup ginger ale

Combine all ingredients except ginger ale. Just add ginger ale and ice before serving. Serves 2.

Lime Egg Cream

1½ cups milk
½ lime soft drink
4 tbsps chocolate syrup

Pour half the milk into each cup. Top with the lime soda so that the foam reaches the top of the glass. Place a spoon in the glass. Add 2 tablespoons of the chocolate syrup per glass hitting the bottom of the spoon if possible. Beat quickly a few times to blend the syrup into the milk without deflating the foam Serves 2.

Liquado Mexicano

½ cup uncooked white rice
1 sticks cinnamon
¼ cup slivered almonds
2 cups water

2 tbsps honey
2–3 drops vanilla extract
½ cup plain yoghurt

Grind rice to a coarse meal in a blender. Mix together rice, cinnamon, almonds and water. Cover loosely and let stand overnight. Purée the rice mixture, then strain. Return to blender, Mix in honey, vanilla extract and yoghurt. Blend until smooth and serve. Serves 2.

Lime Egg Cream

Liquado Mexicano

Spicy Banana Flip

1½ cups milk
1 banana
3 pinches cinnamon
pinch of nutmeg
pinch of ground cloves

extra pinch of nutmeg to garnish
pinch of powdered cardamom
1 raw egg yolk
2 tsps honey
4 ice cubes

Place all ingredients in blender; blend until smooth. Pour into chilled glass and serve topped with a sprinkle of nutmeg. Serves 2.

Tiramisu Smoothie

½ cup milk
½ tsp decaffeinated instant
  coffee granules
1 banana
2 Italian finger biscuit, crushed

½ cup plain yoghurt
½ tsp chocolate sauce
2–3 drops vanilla essence
4 ice cubes

Place all ingredients except 1 biscuit in blender; blend until smooth. Pour into chilled glass and serve topped with more crushed biscuit. Serves 2.

Spicy Banana Flip

Tiramisu Smoothie

Party Snacks

Cheese Triangles

10 oz/300g ricotta cheese
10 oz/300g feta cheese
4 eggs
white pepper
1 packet filo pastry
4 oz/125g melted butter

Pre-heat oven to 400°F/200°C. Combine the ricotta, feta and eggs in a bowl and mix well. Season with pepper. Brush one layer of filo pastry with melted butter, and place another layer on top. Cut the pastry, lengthwise, into 4 strips. To shape the triangles, place a heaped teaspoon of cheese mixture close to the bottom of the right hand corner of the strip. Fold this corner, diagonally across to the left-hand edge over the mixture to form a triangle. Continue folding from right to left in a triangular shape to the end of strip. Brush top of triangle with the melted butter and place on a baking tray. Repeat until all mixture has been used. Bake triangles in the oven for about 20 minutes or until they are golden. Makes 4.

Cheese Triangles

Cheesy Swirls

Cheesy Swirls

14 oz/400g shortcrust pastry
$3\frac{1}{2}$ oz/100g mature cheddar, grated
2 tbsps freshly grated Parmesan cheese
2 tbsps tomato purée
$\frac{1}{2}$ tsp sugar
plain flour for dusting
1 medium egg, beaten, for glazing
vegetable oil for greasing

Preheat the oven to 375°F/190°C. Roll out the pastry on a floured surface and cut to make 2 rectangles measuring 8 x 10in/20 x 25cm. Mix together the cheddar and Parmesan, then set aside. Spread 1 sheet of pastry with the tomato purée mixed with the half teaspoon of sugar. Place the second sheet of pastry on top, then sprinkle with the cheese. Roll up the pastry from the shorter side with the filling inside. Brush the roll with the egg and refrigerate for 20 minutes. Cut the roll into 1cm slices and place on greased baking sheets. Bake for 20 minutes or until golden. Leave on wire racks to cool slightly. Makes 10.

Chicken Nuggets

Chicken Nuggets

1lb/500g chicken mince
1 egg, lightly beaten
1½ oz/45g breadcrumbs, made from
stale bread
2 oz/60g cottage cheese, mashed
4 oz/125g dried breadcrumbs
vegetable oil for shallow frying

Place chicken mince, egg, soft breadcrumbs and cottage cheese in a
bowl and mix well to combine. Take 2 tablespoons of mixture, shape
into a ball, then flatten slightly and gently press into dried breadcrumbs
to coat. Repeat until all remaining mixture is used. Heat ½ in/1 cm oil
in a frying pan over a medium heat until hot, add nuggets and cook
for 2 minutes each side or until cooked through and golden. Drain on
absorbent paper, cool slightly and serve. Makes 24.

Corn Plants

3 red capsicums
3 yellow capsicums
3 tbsps balsamic vinegar
$\frac{1}{2}$ cup olive oil
6 baby corn cobs
1 large onion, chopped
2 cloves garlic, chopped
7 oz/200g minced lamb
3 tsps tomato paste
3 oz/90g bulgur (cracked wheat)
2 cups lamb stock
3 oz/90g frozen peas
3 oz/90g dried apricots, chopped
3 tsps ground coriander
black pepper
watercress sprigs to garnish

Preheat oven to 400°F/200°C. Slice off and discard the tops of the capsicums and deseed. Square off the bottoms and stand on a baking tray lined with a sheet of baking paper. Sprinkle with the balsamic vinegar and 1 tablespoon of the oil. Cook for 15 minutes then add the baby corn to the sheet. Cook for 5–10 minutes, until everything is tender. Meanwhile, heat the remaining oil in a large saucepan, add the onion and garlic and fry for 5 minutes or until softened. Add the minced lamb and cook for 5 minutes on a low heat or until browned. Stir in the tomato paste, bulgur, stock, peas, apricots and coriander, then season. Bring to the boil, then simmer for 15 minutes or until the stock has been absorbed. Stir occasionally. Place the capsicums on plates and fill with the lamb mixture. Insert a baby corn cob and decorate a few watercress sprigs on the top of each one. Serves 6.

Corn Plants

Crunchy Cutlets

Crunchy Cutlets

6 lamb cutlets, trimmed and slightly flattened
1 tbsp vegetable oil

Crunchy coating
1 egg, lightly beaten
¾ cup breadcrumbs, made from stale bread
1 oz/30g cornflakes, crushed

Place egg in a shallow dish. Place breadcrumbs and crushed cornflakes in a separate dish and mix to combine. Dip cutlets in egg, then in breadcrumb mixture to coat. Heat oil in a frying pan over a medium heat until hot, add cutlets and cook for 2 minutes on each side or until cooked through and golden. Serves 6.

Sausage Puffs

Sausage Puffs

12 oz/340g prepared puff pastry
curried sausage filling
12 oz/340g sausage mince
1 small carrot, finely grated
1 tbsp fruit chutney
1 tsp curry powder
freshly ground black pepper
salt

To make filling, place mince, carrot, chutney, salt and black pepper
to taste in a bowl and mix to combine. Cover and refrigerate until
required. Roll out pastry to $1/8$in/3mm thick and cut out a 12in/30cm
square. Cut pastry square in half. Divide filling into two equal portions
then shape each into a thin sausage about 12in/30cm long. Place a
sausage on the long edge of each pastry rectangle and roll up. Brush
edges with water to seal. Cut each roll into $1/2$in/1cm thick slices, place
on greased baking trays and bake for 12–15 minutes or until filling is
cooked and pastry is golden and puffed. Makes 48.

Note: These savoury puffs can be prepared to the baking stage earlier
in the day. Cover with plastic food wrap and store in the refrigerator
until required, then bake as directed in the recipe.

Apple Crumble

Apple Crumble

3 apples

Crumble topping
¾ cup brown sugar
½ cup plain flour
¾ cup rolled oats
2 oz/60g butter

Preheat oven to 350°F/180°C. Cut apples into quarters. Peel and cut out cores. Slice thinly. Place apple slices in lightly buttered ovenproof dish. Make topping. Place sugar, flour and rolled oats in bowl. Chop butter into pieces. Add to bowl. Using your fingers, mix in butter until mixture is crumbly. Sprinkle topping over apples. Bake for 35 minutes. Serves 6.

Apple Roll-ups

2 oz/60g plain flour
5 fl oz/150mL full-fat milk
1 medium egg
rind of 1 orange, finely grated
1 oz/30g butter, melted, plus extra for frying
maple syrup to serve

For the filling
2 eating apples, peeled, cored and chopped
½ tsp ground cinnamon
1 tbsp water

To make the batter, blend the flour, milk, egg, orange rind and melted butter until smooth in a food processor or by using a hand blender. Leave the mixture to rest for 20 minutes. Meanwhile, make the filling. Put the apples, cinnamon and 1 tablespoon of water into a small saucepan, cover, and cook gently for 5–7 minutes, stirring occasionally, until the apples have softened. Melt just enough butter to cover the base of a 18cm non-stick frying pan. Pour in a quarter of the batter and tilt the pan so that it covers the base. Cook for 1–2 minutes on each side, until golden. Keep warm and repeat to make 3 more pancakes, greasing the pan when necessary. Place 2 pancakes on each plate. Fill with the apple mixture and carefully roll up. Serve with maple syrup. Try them with a scoop of vanilla ice cream. Serves 2.

Apple Roll-ups

Fruit and Jelly Wedges

Fruit and Jelly Wedges

14 oz/440g canned fruit of your choice in unsweetened juice
2 tbsps gelatine dissolved in $\frac{1}{2}$ cup hot water, cooled
food colouring of your choice (optional)
3–4 oranges

Drain canned fruit and reserve juice. Combine gelatine mixture and
reserved juice in a measuring jug and make up to 2 cups with water.
Add a few drops of food colouring, if desired. Stir well to combine,
then refrigerate until mixture just begins to thicken. Cut oranges in
half and scoop out pulp with a spoon, leaving orange shells intact.
Fold drained fruit into jelly and spoon mixture into orange shells. Place
shells on a tray and refrigerate for 2–3 hours or until jelly is set. To
serve, cut each jelly-filled orange shell into three wedges. Serves 6–8.

Lamingtons

1 butter or sponge cake, 7 x 11in/18 x 28cm
1 lb/500g icing sugar
3 tbsps cocoa powder
6–8 tbsps warm water
1 lb/500g desiccated coconut

Cut sponge into twelve squares. Set aside. Place icing sugar and cocoa powder in sifter or sieve. Sift into large bowl. Stir in water until you have a runny icing. Pour icing into shallow cake tins. Place coconut in the another tin. Using tongs or two forks, dip cake squares in chocolate icing. Remove cake from icing. Allow excess icing to drain off. Roll in chocolate-coated coconut. Place lamingtons on wire rack to set. Makes 12.

Lammingtons

Syrup Bananas

Syrup Bananas

2 oz/60g unsalted butter
1/3 cup brown sugar
1/2 tsp ground cinnamon
4 bananas, halved lengthwise
1/4 cup banana-flavoured syrup
1/2 cup orange juice
4 scoops vanilla ice cream

Melt butter in a heavy-based saucepan over a medium heat, add sugar
and cinnamon and cook, stirring, until sugar melts and mixture is
combined. Stir in orange juice and banana-flavoured syrup. Cook for
5 minutes or until mixture is thick and syrupy. Add bananas and toss
to coat with syrup. To serve, divide bananas and ice cream between
serving plates and drizzle sauce from pan over ice cream. Serve
immediately. Serves 4.

Notes

Notes

Notes

Notes

Index